D1456572

THE
NBA
A HISTORY OF HOOPS

Published by Creative Education
P.O. Box 227, Mankato, Minnesota 56002
Creative Education is an imprint of The Creative Company
www.thecreativecompany.us

Design and production by Christine Vanderbeek
Art direction by Rita Marshall

Printed by Corporate Graphics in the United States of America

Photographs by Corbis (Owaki-Kulla), Dreamstime (Munktcu), Getty Images
(Andrew D. Bernstein/NBAE, Gary Dineen/NBAE, James Drake/Sports
Illustrated, Stephen Dunn, Focus on Sport, Noah Graham/NBAE, Andy Hayt/
NBAE, Kent Horner/NBAE, Melissa Majchrzak/NBAE, NBA Photos/NBAE,
Greg Nelson/Sports Illustrated, Chuck Pefley, Dick Raphael/NBAE, Edward
Rosenberger, SM/AIUEO, Rocky Widner/NBAE), iStockphoto (Brandon
Laufenberg), US Presswire (Cary Edmondson)

Library of Congress Cataloging-in-Publication Data
LeBoutillier, Nate.
The story of the Utah Jazz / by Nate LeBoutillier.
p. cm. — (The NBA: a history of hoops)
Includes index.
Summary: The history of the Utah Jazz professional basketball
team from its start in New Orleans, Louisiana, in 1974 to today,
spotlighting the franchise's greatest players and moments.
ISBN 978-1-58341-964-9
1. Utah Jazz (Basketball team)—History—Juvenile literature. 2. Basketball—Utah—
Salt Lake City—History—Juvenile literature. I. Title. II. Series.
GV885.52.U8L43 2010   796.323'6409792258—dc22   2009036119

CPSIA: 120109 PO1093

First Edition
2 4 6 8 9 7 5 3 1

Page 3: Guard Deron Williams
Pages 4–5: Forward Mehmet Okur

THE STORY OF THE

UTAH
JAZZ

NATE LeBOUTILLIER

CREATIVE ☾ EDUCATION

CONTENTS

CHAPTER ONE

A TALE OF TWO CITIES

At first glance, Salt Lake City, Utah, and New Orleans, Louisiana, have virtually nothing in common. Salt Lake City lies in the mountain and high desert terrain of the American West and was founded by Brigham Young, a leader of the religious group called the Church of Jesus Christ of Latter-day Saints, or the Mormon Church. New Orleans lies in bayou territory deep in the South, was founded by French explorers, and is considered the birthplace of jazz music. Yet both cities have been home to the same National Basketball Association (NBA) franchise. That team moved to Utah's quiet capital in 1979 and quickly turned Salt Lake City into a basketball town, but the Jazz started out in New Orleans in 1974. The team's owners were determined to make the Jazz like New Orleans itself—colorful and entertaining. With that in mind, one of their first decisions was to deck out the team in uniforms bearing the colors of the city's famous Mardi Gras festival: purple, green, and gold.

Known as a sports and skiing hotspot, Salt Lake City was given a global introduction when it played host to the 2002 Winter Olympic Games.

JAZZ

07

ince New Orleans's 40,000-seat Louisiana Superdome was still a
year away from completion, the first-year Jazz split their home games
between Municipal Auditorium, an opera house where Mardi Gras
balls were held, and Loyola Fieldhouse, which had an elevated playing
floor that required a net around the court to help keep players safe. Both
venues seated fewer than 7,000. The Jazz's inaugural season got off to
a rough start when the team lost its first 11 games. New Orleans's initial
victory came in front of just 5,465 fans at Municipal Auditorium. Down
101–100 to the Portland Trail Blazers with time running out, guard Pete
Maravich hit the winning jump shot. "I went out of bounds, the shot went
through, and the game was over," recalled Maravich, who emerged as the
franchise's first star. "You'd have thought we'd won the world championship that night."

Known to fans as "Pistol Pete," Maravich was one of the game's greatest showmen, and his speed and flair for ball handling were unmatched.
Even before going pro, the Pennsylvania native had won many new basketball fans in the South with a stellar playing career at Louisiana State
University that ended with his setting the National Collegiate Athletic

Association (NCAA) record for points scored. Maravich's LSU team didn't always win, but it did draw fans, and Jazz ownership—sensing he could do the same for New Orleans's new franchise—had made him the first official player in franchise history by trading multiple draft picks to the Atlanta Hawks for him. "We were bringing home the favorite son," said Barry Mendelson, the Jazz's first vice president of business operations. "[Maravich] became a promotional and marketing imperative."

Just three games—all losses—after their first victory, the Jazz fired coach Scotty Robertson and replaced him with Butch van Breda Kolff. Although Maravich was filling up the hoop with help from big men Neal Walk and Mel Counts, things didn't get better, and the Jazz won only 3 more times in their next 23 games to move to 4–34. But van Breda Kolff's

ACQUIRED FROM THE ATLANTA HAWKS IN A TRADE IN 1974, "PISTOL PETE" MARAVICH BECAME THE VERY FIRST PLAYER IN JAZZ HISTORY. Maravich, whom many considered a magician with the basketball, raised basketball awareness wherever he dribbled, passed, or shot, from Baton Rouge (where he played college ball) to Atlanta to New Orleans to Salt Lake City. Maravich seemed especially magical when running the fast break. "If there were five fast breaks, he'd throw five different passes—some with topspin, some with backspin or sidespin," said guard Jimmy McElroy, a Jazz teammate. "My favorite was his pass between the legs, where he'd jump up and whip it through the legs to you." In one of his first seasons with the Jazz, Maravich went through training camp with the local pro football team, the New Orleans Saints. He came back 10 pounds heavier and much stronger, going lift-for-lift with the football linemen in the weight room. "Pete was a masochist," said former Jazz coach Butch van Breda Kolff. "He didn't mind working, working, working." Maravich died of a heart attack at age 40 while playing a game of pickup basketball in 1988.

INTRODUCING...

PETE MARAVICH

POSITION GUARD
HEIGHT 6-FOOT-5
JAZZ SEASONS 1974–80

ON NOVEMBER 5, 1975, A RAIN-STORM OF BIBLICAL PROPORTIONS SPILLED FROM THE LOUISIANA SKY, FLOODING STREETS AND PUTTING THE CITY OF NEW ORLEANS INTO A SORT OF NAUTICAL GRIDLOCK. Jazz players didn't know whether to head to the arena for that evening's game in their cars or by boat. The opening tip was delayed 30 minutes, but by the time a rain-soaked crowd of 26,511 finally made its way into the Louisiana Super-dome to see the second-year Jazz take on the Los Angeles Lakers and center Kareem Abdul-Jabbar, an NBA single-game attendance record had been set. The new record eclipsed the old mark of 20,239, set the previous season in Cleveland when the Cavaliers played the New York Knicks. "It might've been 30,000 if we hadn't had the greatest rain since Noah's Ark," said Jazz star guard Pete Maravich, who posted 30 points, 7 assists, and 5 rebounds on the night to lead New Orleans to a thrilling 113–110 victory. The Jazz would go on to draw a new franchise-record crowd of 35,077 on November 30, 1977, in a 117–114 loss to the Philadelphia 76ers.

COURTSIDE STORIES

RAINDROPS KEEP FALLING

A rainy night in New Orleans.

charges fared better in the season's second half, even winning six in a row in February, and the Jazz finished their inaugural season 23–59.

In the Jazz's second season, the team improved by an NBA-best 15 wins over the previous year but went just 5–13 when Maravich was out of the lineup with injuries. It wasn't until the 1976–77 season, when New Orleans acquired high-scoring swingman Gail Goodrich to complement Maravich, that Jazz fans had legitimate playoff hopes. The two scored a combined 51 points in the Jazz's home opener, a 109–91 win over the Hawks, and New Orleans streaked to a 6–1 record. But van Breda Kolff expected more. "It's not enough for Pete and Gail to make each other better," the coach said. "They've got to make the rest of the team better, too."

Van Breda Kolff led the 1976–77 Jazz to a 14–12 start before he was fired, due largely to a revolt by the club's players. In the players' first game free of van Breda Kolff's domineering coaching style, Maravich played all but 30 seconds in a win versus the Kansas City Kings and scored a new career high of 51 points.

Elgin Baylor, a former NBA scoring dynamo who had once netted 71 points in a single game, was named New Orleans's new coach and got along better with the players, but an injury to Goodrich derailed any postseason aspirations for the Jazz. Prior to the 1977–78 season, the Jazz acquired Leonard "Truck" Robinson, a rugged rebounder and powerful scorer formerly with the Hawks. "He is exactly what this team has never had," said Maravich. "We need rebounds to run, and we need to run to win."

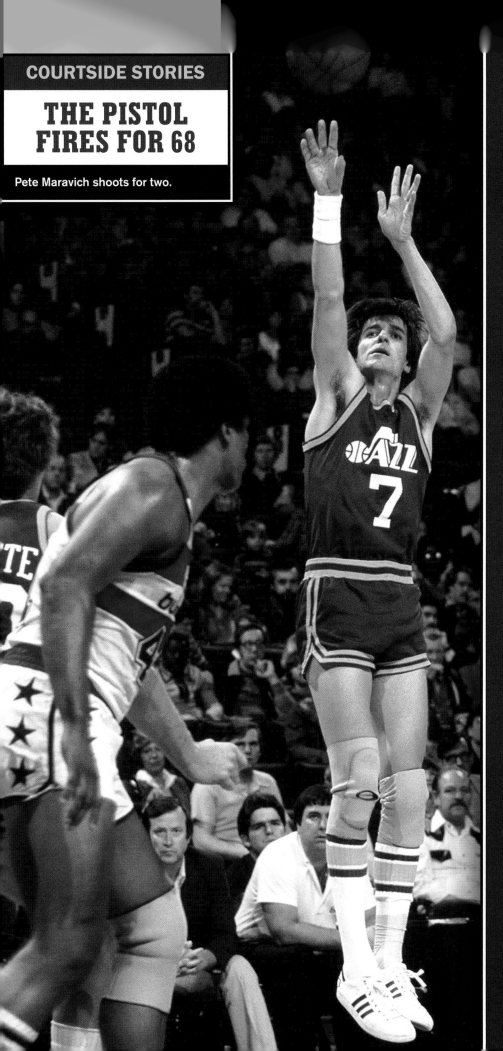

THE PISTOL FIRES FOR 68

Pete Maravich shoots for two.

"PISTOL PETE" MARAVICH WAS A SCORING WIZARD. On February 25, 1977, in a game against the Knicks, the Jazz star scored 48 points before the fourth quarter had even begun. A teammate told him, "You better get a new firing pin, Pistol, 'cause you're wearing that one out." But Maravich kept on firing, scoring 20 more points in the fourth quarter for a franchise record of 68 points. After the game, a 124–107 victory for New Orleans, Maravich wasn't completely satisfied. "I could have scored more," he said. He may have been right. No three-point line existed in the NBA in those days, and Maravich was disqualified on fouls with two minutes remaining, the last two fouls on driving layups over defenders that were waived off by highly questionable offensive-charging calls. "His performance was the best I've ever seen by a guard," said Knicks coach Red Holzman. Press Maravich, Pete's father, said, "I'm glad he was one short of his best effort at LSU [a 69-point outing as a collegian]. It gives him something to shoot for."

IN LATE JANUARY 1978, THE NEW ORLEANS JAZZ'S EFFORT LEVEL AND POPULARITY AMONG LOCAL FANS WAS AT ITS ZENITH. The team had won eight games in a row, a first-ever playoff berth was in sight, and New Orleans fans were flocking to games in record numbers. This up-swing coincided with the career-best play of the club's top star, guard Pete Maravich. "Quite honestly, he was the best player in the league," Jazz center Rich Kelley later recalled. "He became less showy and so much stronger." But on January 31, in a game against the Buffalo Braves, one play changed the franchise's course when Maravich went airborne to execute one of his famous behind-the-back, between-the-legs passes to streaking Jazz guard Aaron James. The play went off as Maravich planned, but he landed awkwardly, tearing cartilage in his right knee. Without Maravich, the Jazz took a nosedive in the standings. With Pistol Pete gone and wins few, New Orleans fans stopped coming to games. And without fans paying for tickets, the team began to lose money. Eighteen months after Maravich's injury, the Jazz relocated to Salt Lake City.

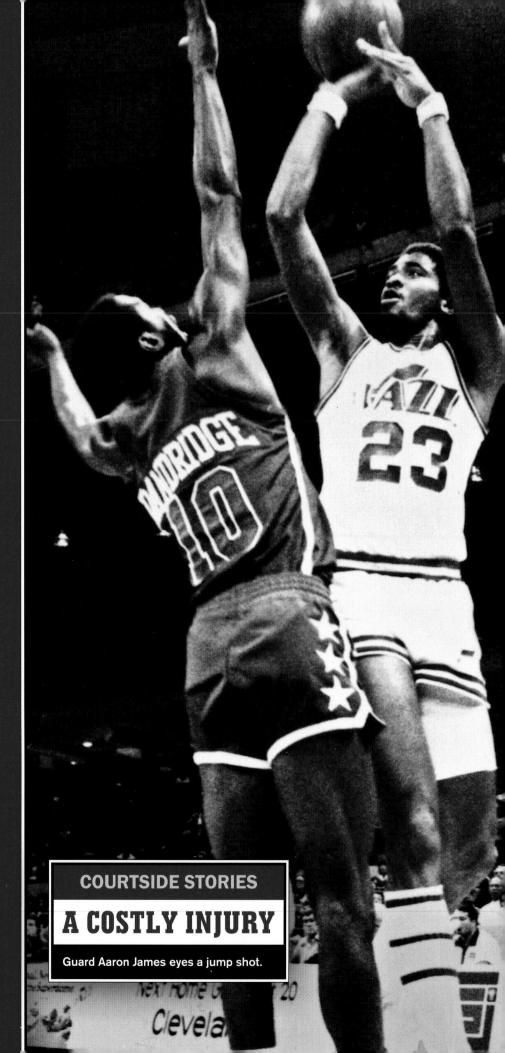

COURTSIDE STORIES
A COSTLY INJURY
Guard Aaron James eyes a jump shot.

The Jazz remained inconsistent, prone to both winning and losing streaks, but they put on quite a show, and fans took notice. A franchise-record 35,077 fans turned up at the Superdome for a game versus the Philadelphia 76ers on November 30, 1977, that ended in a 3-point Jazz loss. More than 31,000 watched New Orleans's club beat Los Angeles just before Christmas. In January, the team went on a nine-game winning streak.

Then Maravich injured his knee. Although his teammates rallied to win the next game, the Jazz lost the following eight contests, and a discouraging atmosphere set in. "I'd come in, play 45 minutes, we'd get our tails kicked, nobody would give a damn," said Robinson. "Then I'd go home and come back again for the same routine."

With Maravich out, crowds at home games dwindled, and the team's play took a dive. The Jazz finished the 1977–78 season 39–43 and missed the playoffs yet again. The next season, with Maravich gimpy and fan support waning, the Jazz slipped to 26–56 ... and soon slipped right on out of town. It seemed there was no money to be made from pro basketball in New Orleans.

CHAPTER TWO

HAVE JAZZ, WILL TRAVEL

Jazz owners, with the NBA's approval, designated Salt Lake City as the club's new destination and moved there in 1979. The people of Utah were no strangers to pro basketball. In the late 1960s and early '70s, Salt Lake City had been home to the Utah Stars of the American Basketball Association (ABA). The Stars franchise folded in 1975, but Jazz owners still felt confident Utah could support a team.

Determined to get off to a better start in Utah than they had in New Orleans, Jazz management made two key leadership changes. Baylor was fired as coach, and former Stars coach Tom Nissalke was hired in his place. Frank Layden, a big man known for his sense of humor, was also hired as the team's new general manager. "My first reaction was that this was not going to be a good move," Layden said. "I didn't think it was a good idea. But it was a job. I thought, 'Hey, if they don't make it here, they can move the team farther west.'"

Guard Carl Nicks and the relocated Jazz started a hot 12–6 in 1980–81 but went cold after that, losing 15 of 17 games during one stretch.

The team still had the popular Maravich on the roster to help draw a crowd, and one of Layden's first moves was to trade for 6-foot-5 forward Adrian Dantley, a potent low-post scorer. The Jazz won their first game in Utah, downing the San Diego Clippers in an exciting 110–109 contest. No one could stop Dantley in 1979–80, as the forward led the Jazz with 28 points per game and was named an NBA All-Star. "We love him," said Layden of Dantley. "He's our piranha. He'll eat you alive."

Maravich, though, was still bothered by a bum knee, and he played in just 17 games that season and saw his scoring average slip to 17.1 points per game. After the season, Utah released him. But the team soon got a boost from highflying young guard Darrell Griffith, an excellent shooter. As Layden once said, "Griffith could shoot from the shores of the Great Salt Lake and probably make it."

Despite the fine play of Dantley and Griffith, the Jazz had their share of problems in the early 1980s. Guard Bernard King, an explosive scorer, played only 19 games in a Jazz uniform due to substance abuse and other off-court troubles, and promising guard Terry Furlow died in a car accident in 1980. Nissalke was fired as head coach in 1981 and replaced by Layden. The Jazz, short on cash, traded the rights to their top 1982 NBA Draft pick, forward Dominique Wilkins, to Atlanta for forwards John

Drew, Freeman Williams, and $1 million. Wilkins would go on to a Hall of Fame NBA career, while Drew and Williams would struggle with substance abuse problems.

Nine seasons into their NBA existence, the Jazz had yet to make the playoffs, but in 1983–84, the franchise's fortunes finally turned. Utah surged to a 45–37 record, won its first Midwest Division title, and finally earned a berth in the Western Conference playoffs. Not only that, but four Jazz players finished the season as NBA statistical leaders: Dantley in scoring, Griffith in three-point shooting, guard Rickey Green in steals, and towering center Mark Eaton in blocks. This talented squad beat the Denver Nuggets in the opening round of the postseason but fell to the Phoenix Suns in round two.

Utah earned solid records again the next two seasons but never truly contended for the league championship. The team needed new talent,

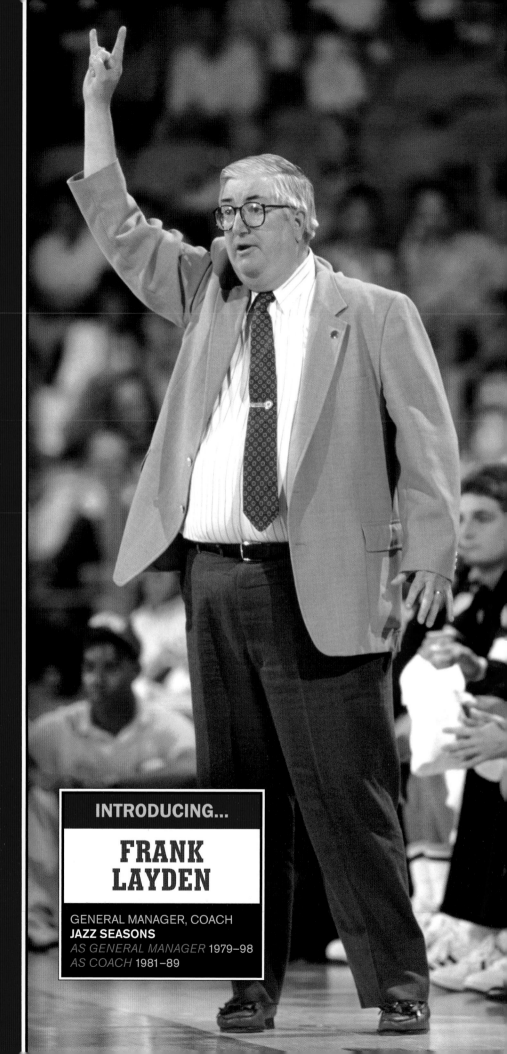

WHEN FRANK LAYDEN, A NEW YORK NATIVE, ARRIVED ON THE SCENE IN UTAH IN 1979 TO TAKE OVER AS THE JAZZ'S GENERAL MANAGER, THE ORGANIZATION WAS WONDERING IF IT HAD MADE A MISTAKE IN RELOCATING FROM NEW ORLEANS. The team's record was poor, and support for basketball in Utah appeared to be minimal. But Layden was instrumental in procuring point guard John Stockton and forward Karl Malone, who became Hall-of-Famers, and he guided the Jazz to their first playoff experience in 1983–84, winning Coach of the Year honors to boot. A wry sense of humor was Layden's calling card. Once, when a fan asked him what time the game started, he replied, "What time can you be there?" Layden was also known for his weight, which hit 335 pounds in the 1980s. He once joked, "I stepped on a scale that gives fortune cards, and the card read, 'Come back in 15 minutes. Alone.'" Layden was known, too, for shooting baskets after games in the darkened arena, alone, a middle-aged man pretending he was an NBA star. Said Layden of his habit, "You have to make life fun."

INTRODUCING...

FRANK LAYDEN

GENERAL MANAGER, COACH
JAZZ SEASONS
AS GENERAL MANAGER 1979–98
AS COACH 1981–89

and in the NBA Drafts of 1984 and 1985, it found two players who would make the Jazz a legitimate force. Those players were point guard John Stockton and forward Karl Malone.

Of the two, Malone had the more immediate impact. At 6-foot-9 and a chiseled 255 pounds, Malone had the look of a football linebacker and the grace of a ballerina. Fans called him "The Mailman," because no matter what the team needed—be it a clutch basket or critical rebound—he always delivered. Malone also delivered excitement in Utah, often finishing fast breaks with a thunderous dunk. "People tend to get out of Karl's way unless they want their careers to be over," Green said.

In 1986, the Jazz decided to make Malone their cornerstone player and traded Dantley to the Detroit Pistons for forward Kelly Tripucka and center Kent Benson. The Mailman immediately assumed command in Utah, leading the team with 21.7 points and 10.4 rebounds per game in 1986–87. The following season, Stockton emerged as a star as well. That year, the 6-foot-1 guard led the NBA in assists with 13.8 per game. Stockton rarely turned the ball over, almost always put his passes to teammates right on the mark, and also played high-energy defense.

During the 1988–89 season, Layden stepped down as Utah's coach and promoted his top assistant, Jerry Sloan, in his place. Behind Coach Sloan, Stockton, and Malone, the Jazz emerged as one of the Western Conference's best teams in the late 1980s and early '90s. From 1988–89 to 1991–92, Utah won more than 50 games every season. But while the regular seasons were rousing successes, the playoffs were a different story. Even with the addition of such players as heady guard Jeff Malone and lithe forward Thurl Bailey, the Jazz made early playoff exits every year.

COURTSIDE STORIES

FANS TURN ON TO JAZZ

The Utah crowd shows its support.

IN 1979, THE NEWLY RELOCATED UTAH JAZZ PLAYED THEIR INITIAL GAMES AT THE SALT PALACE BEFORE PALTRY CROWDS. When the Jazz's play improved in the mid-1980s, more fans showed up. Starting on November 15, 1988, the Jazz sold out every home game. In the fall of 1991, the Jazz opened the new Delta Center (later renamed EnergySolutions Arena), and the sellout streak continued for an impressive 209 straight contests. Over that stretch, the Jazz racked up a 174–35 home record. It was a far cry from the franchise's earliest days playing in New Orleans's cavernous Superdome, which was built more for the football-playing New Orleans Saints. The team's earliest owners tried everything to attract fans, from putting lucky numbers in programs for prize giveaways to holding half-time shooting contests for cash and even cars. Most popular was a promotion that promised free French fries to fans if the Jazz scored 110 points or more. "We could be losing by 20," said former Jazz general manager Barry Mendelson, "but the guys would call timeout to argue over who was going to take the 'free fries' shot."

POSITION FORWARD
HEIGHT 6-FOOT-5
JAZZ SEASONS 1979–86

ADRIAN DANTLEY

ADRIAN DANTLEY WAS UNDERESTIMATED FROM A VERY EARLY AGE. As a 6-foot-4 and 245-pound freshman at DeMatha High School in Hyattsville, Maryland, Dantley was often judged by opposing teams as too fat to be considered a threat. That lasted only until Dantley used his smooth moves and flat-footed but deadeye shooting to torch the opposition. Dantley grew only one inch after that first year of high school, and although he stayed close to the same weight, what once looked like blubber became chiseled brawn. The NBA's 1977 Rookie of the Year with the Buffalo Braves came to the Jazz via trade in 1979. He routinely scored in bunches while shooting a high percentage, sometimes going so far as to chide opponents in doubt of his talents. "After I score on them," Dantley explained with a smile, "I get behind them at the other end of the court, change my voice, and say, 'I wouldn't let no fat boy come inside and pile-drive on me like that.' Then they turn around and see it's me." Dantley was elected to the Basketball Hall of Fame in 2008.

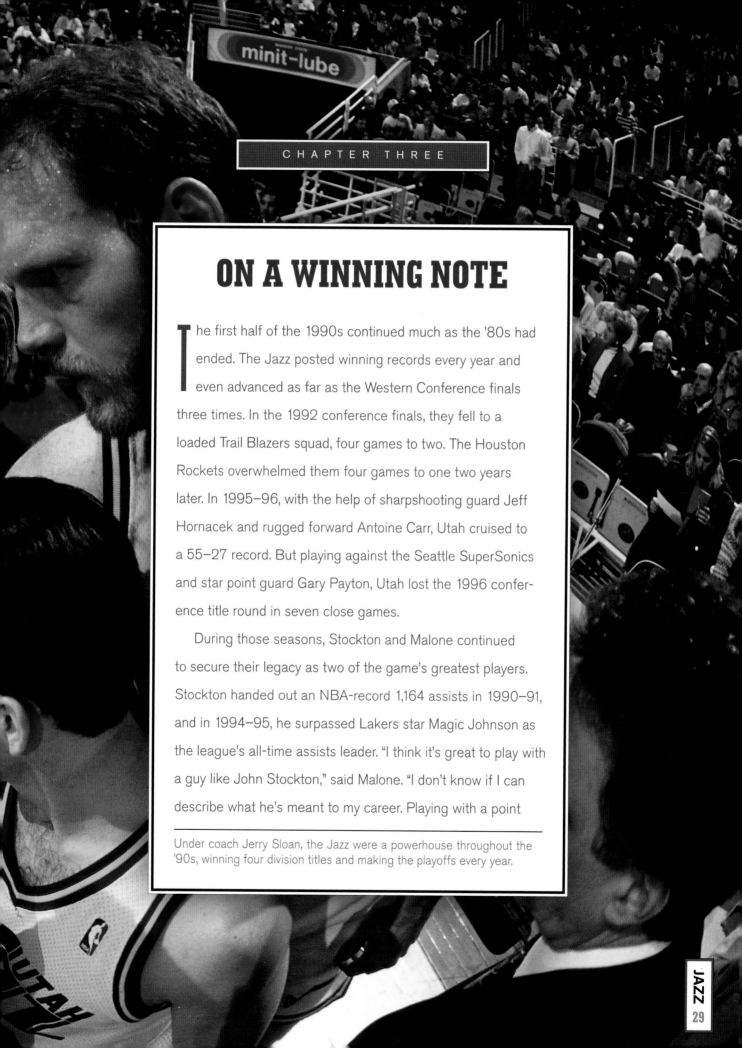

CHAPTER THREE

ON A WINNING NOTE

The first half of the 1990s continued much as the '80s had ended. The Jazz posted winning records every year and even advanced as far as the Western Conference finals three times. In the 1992 conference finals, they fell to a loaded Trail Blazers squad, four games to two. The Houston Rockets overwhelmed them four games to one two years later. In 1995–96, with the help of sharpshooting guard Jeff Hornacek and rugged forward Antoine Carr, Utah cruised to a 55–27 record. But playing against the Seattle SuperSonics and star point guard Gary Payton, Utah lost the 1996 conference title round in seven close games.

During those seasons, Stockton and Malone continued to secure their legacy as two of the game's greatest players. Stockton handed out an NBA-record 1,164 assists in 1990–91, and in 1994–95, he surpassed Lakers star Magic Johnson as the league's all-time assists leader. "I think it's great to play with a guy like John Stockton," said Malone. "I don't know if I can describe what he's meant to my career. Playing with a point

Under coach Jerry Sloan, the Jazz were a powerhouse throughout the '90s, winning four division titles and making the playoffs every year.

guard who truly wants to get his teammates involved before himself—you don't find that much in this league anymore."

or years, critics had said that the Jazz had missed their prime opportunities for an NBA championship and were bound to fall off their winning pace. Utah and its seemingly ageless stars, however, only grew stronger. In 1996–97, The Mailman poured in 27.4 points per game and was named the NBA's Most Valuable Player (MVP), and the Jazz rolled to a 64–18 record—their best mark ever. In the playoffs, they crushed the Los Angeles Clippers and Lakers to reach the Western Conference finals again. This time, the Jazz would not be denied, beating a tough Rockets team to advance to the NBA Finals at last.

In the Finals, the Jazz faced the Chicago Bulls and star guard Michael Jordan. The Bulls won the first two games, but Utah battled back to even the series at two wins apiece. Stockton and Malone repeatedly ran their trademark pick-and-roll play, and young players such as forward Bryon Russell and center Greg Ostertag made big contributions. But Jordan dominated in the next two games to lead Chicago to its fifth NBA championship in seven seasons.

Jeff Hornacek carved out a 14-season NBA career with sharp outside shooting, giving Utah elite three-point marksmanship in the late '90s.

A year later, Utah charged right back to the NBA Finals to again meet the Bulls. The result was identical. With Utah on the ropes in Game 6, Malone played a stellar game. Jordan was even better, though, netting 45 points in the final game of his Bulls career and sinking the winning shot with 6 seconds remaining to give Chicago the title again. "We fought hard," said Malone, who scored 31 points to lead his team yet had the ball stolen from him by Jordan shortly before the Bulls star hit his big shot. "It was a tough loss for us."

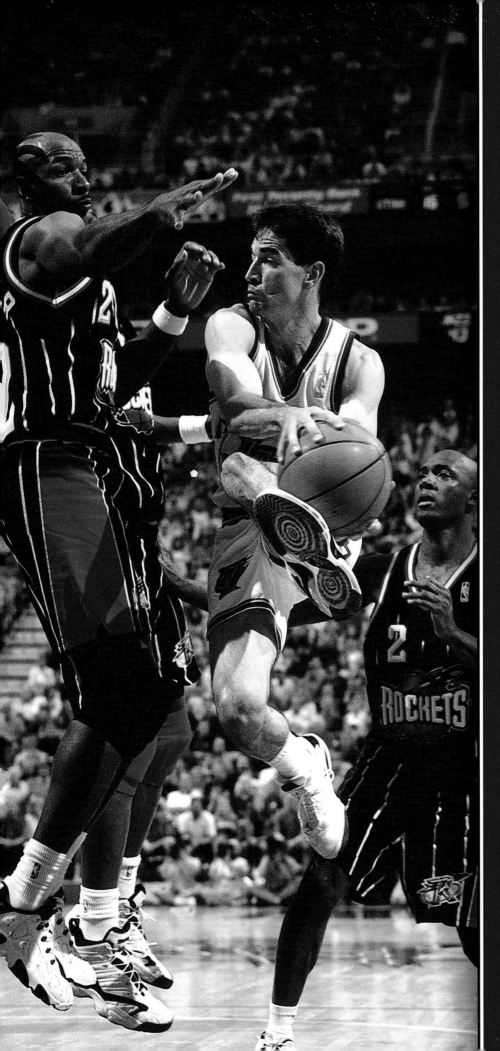

THERE MAY NEVER HAVE BEEN A MORE PERFECT POINT GUARD THAN JOHN STOCKTON. While many point guards do one thing well, such as pass or score or play defense, Stockton excelled at all parts of the job description. Over the course of his 19 seasons in a Jazz uniform, the ordinary-looking Stockton was extraordinary at passing (becoming the all-time league leader in assists), scoring (averaging 13.1 points per game for his career), and playing defense (becoming the all-time NBA leader in steals). Stockton was also incredibly durable, playing every game in 17 of 19 seasons. With Stockton at the point, the Jazz were always winners, making the playoffs in every one of the point guard's seasons. Utah reached the NBA Finals in 1997 and 1998 but lost to Michael Jordan's Chicago Bulls. "A lot of this is about the journey," Stockton said upon retiring in 2003. "I'm sure there are people that have won championships who haven't had to work very hard at it. We worked very hard and haven't done it, and yet I feel a lot of reward out of the effort that it took to compete."

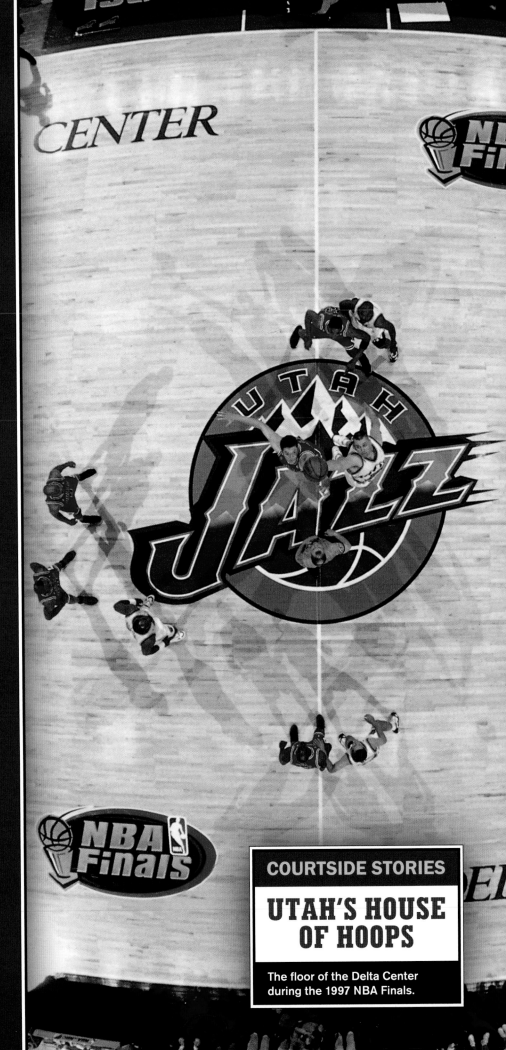

THE JAZZ WERE AN UNSETTLED FRANCHISE IN THEIR EARLY YEARS. In New Orleans, they spent time playing in three different arenas, and after moving to Utah in 1979, they set up shop in the old Salt Palace. They finally found a suitable, permanent home in 1991 when they moved into Salt Lake City's new, state-of-the-art Delta Center. The $93-million arena was funded largely by local businessman Larry Miller, who had taken ownership of the Jazz in 1986, and its high energy level soon helped make the Jazz a steady winner. "On any given night, the Delta Center becomes its own city with 20,000 energetic fans alongside ushers, catering, security, police, paramedics, and media," said Jazz executive Dennis Haslam. "It's a loud, noisy place. Jazz fans love it. And our opponents often find it intimidating." In 2006, the building was renamed EnergySolutions Arena, but many local fans continued to refer to the house of hoops by its original name. The name change prompted no change in the Jazz's home-court advantage, either. In 2009–10, the team went 32–9 in the house Miller built.

COURTSIDE STORIES

UTAH'S HOUSE OF HOOPS

The floor of the Delta Center during the 1997 NBA Finals.

After that Finals defeat, many fans wondered if Utah would replace Stockton or Malone with younger talent while the veterans still had trade value. But Jazz president Frank Layden made clear that he intended to keep the team's veterans together for as long as it took. "We want to have statues of John and Karl outside the Delta Center someday," he said. "You'll never see us panic or make changes just to make changes. We do things differently here."

Malone proved that age had not slowed him by winning the league's MVP award again in 1998–99, and the hustling Stockton continued to pace Utah's offense. The pair led Utah to the playoffs every year they played for the Jazz, but after the 2002–03 season, the long marriage ended. Stockton retired, and Malone played the 2003–04 season with the Lakers before retiring at season's end.

FOR NEARLY 20 YEARS IN UTAH, "THE MAILMAN" DELIVERED. It was more than just the 25 points and 10.1 rebounds he averaged per game. It was more, too, than the consistency of showing up season in and season out and missing just 10 games total in his Jazz career. Malone's true value was in his muscle and winning attitude. Sculpted more like a bodybuilder than a basketball player, Malone gave the Jazz an edge in power that said "don't mess with me" without being disrespectful. "He was extremely physical, and at times he was borderline cheap," said Doc Rivers, an NBA guard who played against Malone's Jazz. "But that didn't bother me because he was trying to win." Teamed with resourceful point guard John Stockton—no stranger to physical play himself—for 18 seasons, Malone was a vital part of Jazz consistency that turned the franchise around. "Stockton-to-Malone" became a household phrase for the way Stockton would dish to the Mailman on Utah's famous pick-and-roll play. Malone retired in 2004 trailing only legendary center Kareem Abdul-Jabbar on the all-time NBA scoring list.

CHAPTER FOUR

NEW-AGE JAZZ

After the loss of their longtime stars, the Jazz looked to new-comers such as Andrei Kirilenko, a 6-foot-9 forward from Russia. Other young players such as guard Gordan Giricek and forwards Mehmet Okur, Carlos Boozer, and Matt Harpring also joined the mix. With such an influx of inexperienced youth, the Jazz suffered their first losing season in 20 years in 2004–05. In the 2005 NBA Draft, however, the Jazz found their point guard of the future: Deron Williams. "I'm just honored to play for the Jazz and to play after John Stockton," said the brilliant passer out of the University of Illinois, "to wear the same jersey he wore and be on the same floor he was on."

Deron Williams proved a worthy successor to John Stockton, averaging 16.2 points and 9.3 assists a game by just his second NBA season.

The Jazz improved from 26–56 to an even 41–41 in 2005–06, with Coach Sloan getting much of the credit for conducting the Jazz's turnaround. Sloan had endured the death of his longtime wife, Bobbye, in 2004 and the banter of some critics who claimed that the old-school coach had lost touch with the new generation of NBA players. In 2006–07, Okur and Boozer stepped up their games, and Williams's play flourished as he averaged 16.2 points and 9.3 assists per game. Rookie forwards Ronnie Brewer and Paul Millsap learned the NBA game, and the addition of guard Derek Fisher gave the team the wizened veteran it had been lacking. The 2006–07 Jazz not only went 51–31 and made the playoffs, but they won their first two series and found themselves in the Western Conference finals facing San Antonio.

The Spurs were a deep, fundamentally sound team that had won the NBA championship in 2003 and 2005. The Jazz gave them a run, winning Game 3 at home in front of a rabid Utah crowd, but the Spurs took the next two games to close out the series. The series was a physical one, with some frustrated Jazz players and fans crying foul about San Antonio's bullying style of play. "They came at us really hard," said Sloan

Pages 42–43: Matt Harpring beats the Spurs defense for a bucket.

INTRODUCING...

JERRY SLOAN

COACH
JAZZ SEASONS 1988–PRESENT

JERRY SLOAN MADE A NAME FOR HIMSELF AS A GRITTY, EMOTIONAL PLAYER. As a guard for the Chicago Bulls in the 1960s, Sloan backed down from no one. "In his first year with us, he led the league in floorburns and fights in practice," joked Sloan's Bulls coach, Red Kerr. After Sloan's playing career was over, he still couldn't get the game, or intensity, out of his blood. The Bulls figured his fiery leadership would be a good thing to have on their bench, so they made him head coach in 1979, but Sloan lasted only three seasons. Eventually, Frank Layden, Utah's coach and general manager, lured Sloan to Salt Lake City because of that fire. "I saw how he loved the game and how he related to the players and how the players respected him," Layden said. Sloan guided the Jazz to the NBA Finals in 1997 and 1998, only to lose to—who else?—the Bulls. Sloan celebrated his 20th year as the Jazz's head coach in 2008. During that span, all other NBA franchises had made a combined total of 223 coaching changes.

ON JANUARY 7, 2009, LEGENDARY RADIO AND TV ANNOUNCER ROD HUNDLEY CALLED HIS 3,000TH JAZZ GAME, A 116–90 BLOWOUT VICTORY OVER, IRONICALLY, THE NEW ORLEANS HORNETS, AN NBA FRANCHISE LOCATED IN THE JAZZ'S BIRTH CITY. Hundley, who joined the Jazz organization prior to the team's start in New Orleans in 1974, has worked for the team ever since. Hundley's announcing bag of tricks includes such catchphrases as: "It's in the ol' refrigerator," and "With a gentle push and a mild arc, the old cowhide globe hits home," and "You gotta love it, baby!" Prior to Hundley's Jazz experience, he announced games for the Los Angeles Lakers and Phoenix Suns. Before that, he was a guard for six seasons on Minneapolis and Los Angeles Lakers teams that thrice reached the NBA Finals but lost out to the Boston Celtics each time. When Hundley ended his playing days and hung up his sneakers, he was faced with a tough career decision: go into coaching or start a career in broadcasting. He chose wisely. "Coaches get fired," said Hundley. "Broadcasters don't."

COURTSIDE STORIES

VOICE OF THE JAZZ

Rod Hundley courtside in 2009.

of the Spurs, who went on to sweep the Cleveland Cavaliers in the NBA Finals to win another title. "They destroyed our will to want to play."

The 2007–08 Jazz assembled a mediocre 16–16 record early on. But the team made a trade to acquire long-range marksman Kyle Korver just after Christmas, and the holiday gift propelled the Jazz to a franchise-record-tying 19-game home winning streak. Williams was now one of the NBA's elite point guards, both a heady facilitator of the offense and a lockdown defender. The Jazz again started the playoffs with a bang, downing the Rockets four games to two. But the Lakers, led by star guard Kobe Bryant, eliminated them in the next round.

The Jazz slipped a little in 2008–09, finishing 48–34 and getting knocked out in the first round of the playoffs, again at the hands of the Bryant-led Lakers. But the season offered further glimpses of a promising future. Young guard C. J. Miles stepped into the starting lineup full-time, and the Jazz's top pick in the 2008 NBA Draft, seven-foot center Kosta Koufos, made valuable contributions as a rookie coming off the bench. The youthful Jazz won 53 games in 2009–10 before seeing their season end with a third consecutive playoff defeat to their rivals to the west, the Lakers.

Although the Jazz have yet to win an NBA title, they have assembled the fifth-highest winning percentage in league history. They also have built a history rich in bright stars and numerous close calls with championship glory. For parts of three decades, the franchise's greatest heroes—John Stockton and Karl Malone—rewrote the Utah playbook with their effort and chemistry. Future Jazz players need only read and practice it to ensure more beautiful basketball in Utah.

The youthful energy of C. J. Miles (below) and Kosta Koufos (opposite) helped Utah make a fourth straight playoff appearance in 2010.

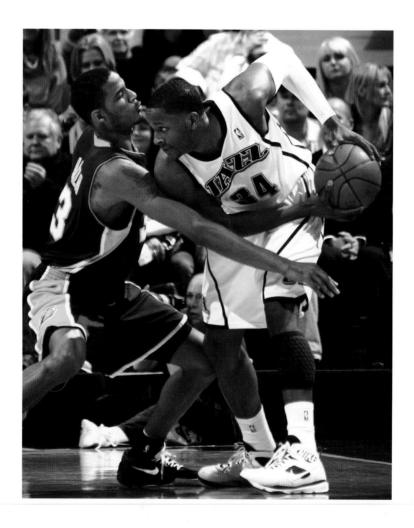

INDEX